Welcome to the real
world —

Good luck.

Mommy + Melly

ESSENTIAL 20s

ESSENTIAL 20s

20 ESSENTIAL ITEMS FOR EVERY ROOM IN A 20-SOMETHING'S FIRST PLACE

Illustrations by Lizzy Stewart

CHRONICLE BOOKS

SAN FRANCISCO

Library of Congress Cataloging-in-Publication Data

Names: Stewart, Lizzy, author illustrator.
Title: Essential 20s /
    illustrations by Lizzy Stewart.
Other titles: Essential twenties
Description: San Francisco, California : Chroncle Books, [2018]
Identifiers: LCCN 2017014565 | ISBN 9781452164304 (hc : alk. paper)
Subjects: LCSH: Home economics—Equipment and supplies—Pictorial works. |
    Home economics—Equipment and supplies—Registers.
Classification: LCC TX299 .S74 2017 | DDC 640—dc23 LC record available at https://lccn.loc.gov/2017014565

Manufactured in China

Design by Rachel Harrell

10 9 8 7 6 5 4 3

Chronicle books and gifts are available at special quantity discounts to corporations, professional associations, literacy programs, and other organizations. For details and discount information, please contact our corporate/premiums department at corporatesales@chroniclebooks.com or at 1-800-759-0190.

Chronicle Books LLC
680 Second Street
San Francisco, California 94107
www.chroniclebooks.com

CONTENTS

INTRODUCTION

Congratulations! You've moved into your own place!

So . . . now what?

Whether you're moving across the country or just two blocks away, packing up and moving into a new home or apartment is both exhilarating and stressful. Moving out is hard. Moving in is harder. Whether you're adventuring off on your own or moving in with someone or with a group, your home needs to be fully stocked. Kitchens need pots and pans. Bathrooms need toilet paper. Picture frames need to be hung up with a hammer and nails. But where do you even start? You want your home to look like a West Elm ad, but you've got an Ikea budget.

If you're like most people, you may have bunch of extraneous items but few necessary items. Maybe you have a lemon zester and a butter warmer sitting pretty on your counter, but you're stealing plastic spoons from your local bodega. Perhaps you're searching through twenty band T-shirts every morning, trying to find something appropriate for work.

If this sounds like you, don't fret! Here is a guidebook for all the essential twenty items that you need for every part of your home—from your wardrobe to your toolbox and everything in between. These lists will help prevent you from buying excessive items and make sure you only keep the key ones. So drop the herb stripper! Buy that ergonomically friendly set of spoons! Remove the graphic T-shirts from your online shopping cart! And pick up a sensible bath mat and some cotton sheets.

However, this book is by no means a prescription. If you feel like you need less stuff in your home, more power to you. And if you need a few more items for your own comfort, go ahead and keep that lemon zester. This is merely a starting point.

Good luck! Have fun! And remember, Bed Bath and Beyond coupons never expire.

CLOTHING

BASICS — WOMEN

WHITE
T-SHIRT

WHITE BUTTON-UP

BLACK
T-SHIRT

SWEATER

BOOTS

CHAMBRAY SHIRT

BLACK JEANS

BLUE JEANS

LITTLE BLACK
DRESS

BLACK BLAZER

BLUE BLAZER

HEELS

PAJAMAS

SKIRT

FLATS

WORKOUT GEAR

SNEAKERS

BRAS

UNDERWEAR (20 PAIRS)

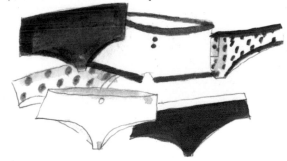

SOCKS (20 PAIRS)

SEASONAL — WOMEN

WINTER

HAT

SCARF

WINTER COAT

GLOVES

COMFY SWEATER

SNOW BOOTS

SPRING

RAINCOAT

LIGHT JACKET

RAIN BOOTS

DENIM JACKET

LONG SLEEVE SHIRT

SUMMER

SHORTS

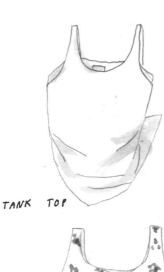

TANK TOP

SANDALS

SWIMSUIT

SUNDRESS

FALL

CARDIGAN

PEA COAT

VEST

FLANNEL SHIRT

BASICS—MEN

WHITE
T-SHIRT

BLACK
T-SHIRT

BLUE BUTTON-UP

SWEATER

WHITE BUTTON-UP

BLACK BLAZER

SUIT

TIE

DRESS-UP SHIRT

BLUE JEANS

LOAFERS

BLACK JEANS

BLUE BLAZER

BOOTS

19

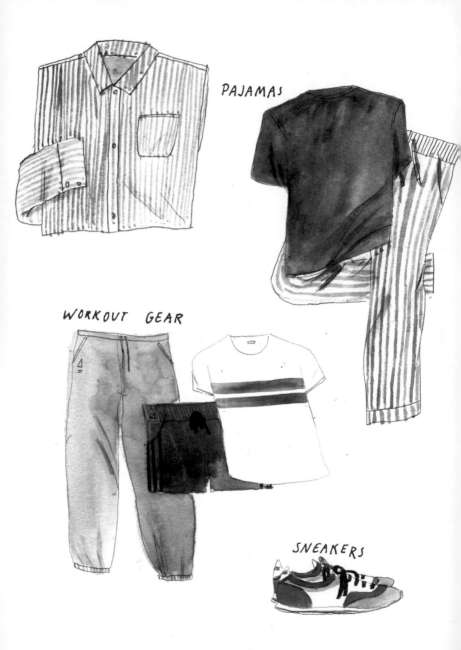

PAJAMAS

WORKOUT GEAR

SNEAKERS

UNDERSHIRT

UNDERWEAR (20 PAIRS)

SOCKS (20 PAIRS)

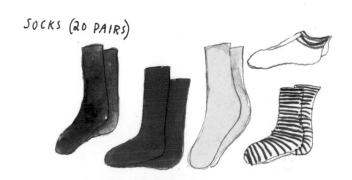

SEASONAL—MEN

WINTER

COMFY SWEATER

GLOVES

HAT

COAT

SCARF

SNOW BOOTS

SPRING

LIGHT JACKET

RAINCOAT

DENIM JACKET

RAIN BOOTS

HENLEY SHIRT

SUMMER

SANDALS

POLO SHIRT

SHORTS

SWIMSUIT

CANVAS SNEAKERS

FALL

FLANNEL SHIRT

PEA COAT

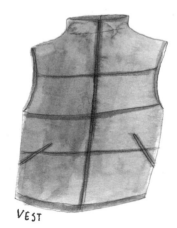

VEST

CARDIGAN

BEDROOM

PILLOW & PILLOWCASE

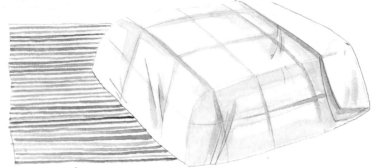

COMFORTER & DUVET COVER

MATTRESS &
BOX SPRING

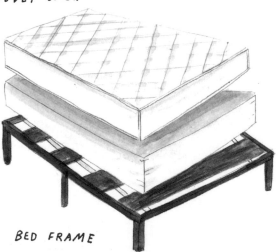

BED FRAME

FITTED SHEET & FLAT SHEET

STORAGE BINS

LAUNDRY HAMPER

DESK

FULL—LENGTH
MIRROR

BLINDS / CURTAINS

ALARM CLOCK

HANGERS

TRASH CAN

MAY

CALENDAR

LAMP

BOOKS

NIGHTSTAND

CHAIR

DRESSER

BATHROOM

TOWELS — BATH & HAND

TOILET BRUSH

BATH MAT

TOILET PAPER

WASHCLOTH/LOOFAH

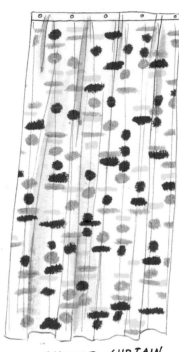

SHOWER CURTAIN

SHOWER CADDY

HAIR
DRYER

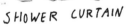

TRASH
CAN

TOILET PLUNGER

SHAVING KIT

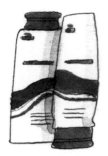

SHAMPOO & CONDITIONER

BAR SOAP / BODY WASH

HAND SOAP

LOTION

DEODORANT

FILM

HAIR PRODUCTS

MAGAZINES

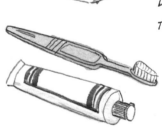

FLOSS

DENTAL HYGIENE—
TOOTHBRUSH, TOOTHPASTE,
MOUTHWASH, FLOSS

HAIRBRUSH/COMB

LIVING ROOM & DINING ROOM

THROW PILLOWS

CHAIR

TV

COUCH

PLANTS

COASTERS

COFFEE TABLE

THROW BLANKET

PAINTINGS / PICTURES

FLOWERS

TV STAND

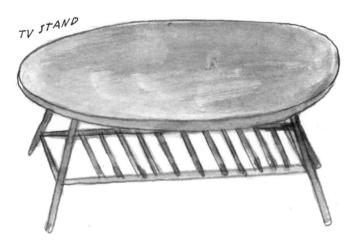

BOOKS

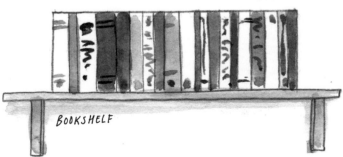

BOOKSHELF

CURTAINS

DVDS

DINING CHAIRS

TABLE

LAMP

NAPKINS

TRIVET

KITCHEN

COUNTER, CUPBOARDS & DRAWERS

CUTLERY

MUGS & GLASSES

WINEGLASSES

BOWLS

PLATES

MICROWAVE

TOASTER

BLENDER

DISH RACK

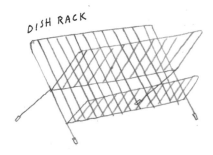

PAPER TOWELS

WATER FILTER

COFFEE MAKER

KETTLE

KITCHEN TOWELS

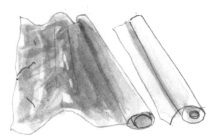
ALUMINUM FOIL AND
PLASTIC WRAP

ICE CUBE TRAY

FOOD STORAGE BAGS

RECYCLING CONTAINER

TRASH CAN

FOOD STORAGE CONTAINERS

COOKWARE & UTENSILS

POTS

PAN

CASSEROLE DISH

BAKING SHEET

MIXING BOWLS

DRY & WET MEASURING CUPS

CUTTING BOARD

MEASURING SPOONS

COLANDER

WHISK

SPATULA

SLOTTED SPOON

WOODEN SPOON

LADLE

VEGETABLE PEELER

CAN OPENER

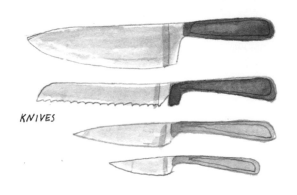

KNIVES

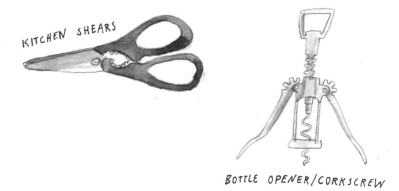

KITCHEN SHEARS

BOTTLE OPENER/CORKSCREW

OVEN MITTS

PANTRY

GARLIC & ONIONS

SPICES

SALT & PEPPER

FLOUR

PLAIN FLOUR

SUGAR

HONEY

VEGETABLE OIL

OLIVE OIL

VINEGAR

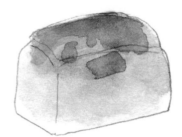

BREAD

SNACKS

PASTA

RICE

OATMEAL

CEREAL

BEANS

CANNED
SOUP/ BROTH

NUT BUTTER

COFFEE/TEA

TOMATO SAUCE

REFRIGERATOR & FREEZER

MILK

JUICE

EGGS

BUTTER

COLD CUTS

LEAFY GREENS

FRUITS

VEGETABLES

CHEESE

YOGURT

HUMMUS

CONDIMENTS

SALAD
DRESSING

JAM

ICE CREAM

ICE

FROZEN VEGGIES

FROZEN FRUIT

MEAT

FISH

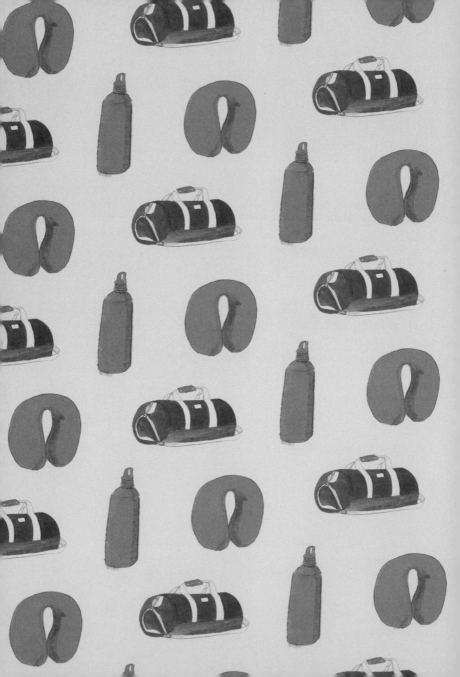

TRAVEL GEAR

LARGE SUITCASE

CARRY-ON SUITCASE

WEEKENDER BAG

BACKPACK

TOILETRY BAG,
WHICH INCLUDES:

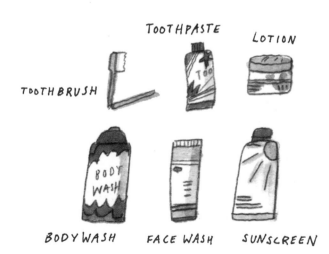

TOOTHBRUSH

TOOTHPASTE

LOTION

BODY WASH

FACE WASH

SUNSCREEN

PACKING BAGS

WATER BOTTLE

MESH BAG FOR
DIRTY CLOTHES

ADAPTER PLUG

PORTABLE
PHONE CHARGER

HEADPHONES

TRAVEL PILLOW

UP-TO-DATE
PASSPORT & ID

READING
MATERIAL

TECHNOLOGY

BATTERIES
(VARIOUS SIZES)

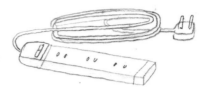

EXTENSION CORDS

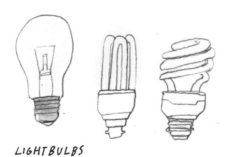

LIGHTBULBS

DVD PLAYER

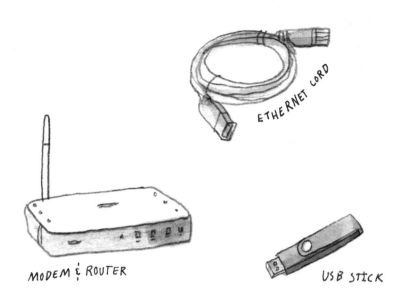

ETHERNET CORD

MODEM & ROUTER

USB STICK

PRINTER

CAMERA

CAMERA MEMORY CARD

CAMERA BATTERY

CAMERA CHARGER

LAPTOP CHARGER

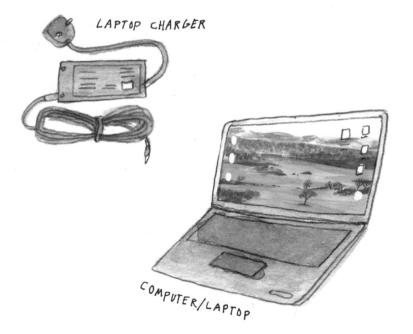

COMPUTER/LAPTOP

SPEAKERS

HEADPHONES

CELL PHONE

CELL PHONE CASE

CELL PHONE CHARGER

PORTABLE PHONE CHARGER

HEALTH & SAFETY

ASPIRIN / IBUPROFEN

BANDAGES & GAUZE PADS

DIGESTIVE MEDICATION

HYDROCORTISONE CREAM /
CALAMINE LOTION

COLD MEDICATION

VITAMINS

BURN GEL

ACE BANDAGES

MEDICAL TAPE

ANTIBIOTIC CREAM

ALLERGY MEDICATION

EYE
DROPS

CONTACT SOLUTION

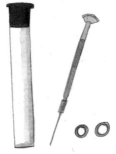

EYEGLASS REPAIR KIT

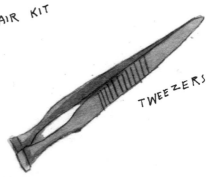

TWEEZERS

THERMOMETER

ICE PACK

PRESCRIPTION
MEDICATIONS

HYDROGEN
PEROXIDE

RUBBING ALCOHOL

CLEANING
SUPPLIES

RUBBER GLOVES

PAPER TOWELS /RAGS

BROOM & DUSTPAN

VACUUM

MOP & BUCKET

CARPET STAIN
REMOVER

CHLORINE BLEACH

MULTI PURPOSE
CLEANER

SHOWER
SCRUBBER

GLASS
CLEANER

DISH DETERGENT

DISHWASHER SOAP

TOILET BOWL
CLEANER

TOILET
SCRUBBER

LAUNDRY DETERGENT

SPONGES

LAUNDRY STAIN
REMOVER

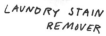

FURNITURE
POLISH

SHOWER / BATH CLEANER

TRASH BAGS

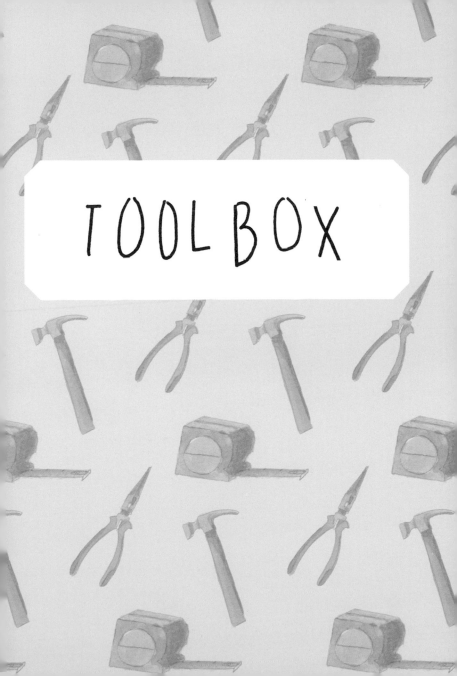

TOOLBOX

HAMMER

FLAT HEAD
SCREWDRIVER

PHILLIPS
SCREWDRIVER

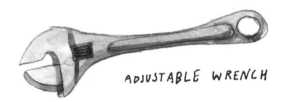

ADJUSTABLE WRENCH

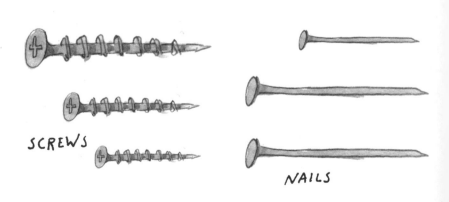

SCREWS

NAILS

TAPE MEASURE

PLIERS

SOCKET WRENCH

ALLEN
WRENCHES

UTILITY KNIFE

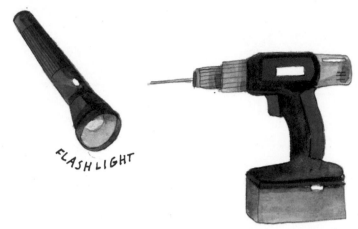

FLASHLIGHT

ELECTRIC DRILL

LEVEL

RULER

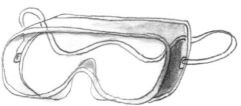

SAFETY GOGGLES

WD-40

CONSTRUCTION
GLOVES

SUPER GLUE

DUCT TAPE

ITEMS YOU SHOULD HAVE EXTRAS OF

TISSUES

LIGHTBULBS

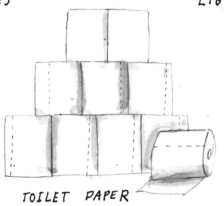

TOSLET PAPER

CANDLES

TOWELS

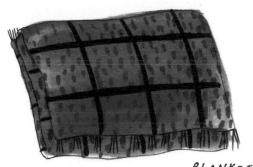

BLANKETS

WATERPROOF
MATCHES

MATCHES

KITCHEN SPONGES

TRASH BAGS

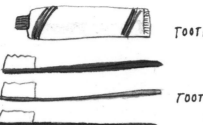

TOOTH PASTE

TOOTH BRUSHES

DISH SOAP

PAPER & NOTE PADS

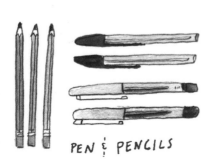

PEN & PENCILS

HAND SOAP

BEDSHEETS & PILLOWCASES

BATTERIES

LIQUOR

WATER FILTERS

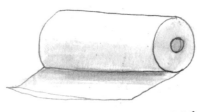

PAPER TOWELS